WORDS ARE IMPORTANT

GRAY BOOK

•

New Revised Edition

•

by Edgar H. Schuster

THIS BOOK IS THE PROPERTY OF:

STATE ____________
PROVINCE ____________
COUNTY ____________
PARISH ____________
SCHOOL DISTRICT ____________
OTHER ____________

Book No. ________
Enter information in one of the spaces to the left as instructed

ISSUED TO	Year Used	CONDITION	
		ISSUED	RETURNED

PUPILS to whom this textbook is issued must not write on any page or mark any part of it in any way, consumable textbooks excepted.

1. Teachers should see that the pupil's name is clearly written in ink in the spaces above in every book issued.
2. The following terms should be used in recording the condition of the book: New; Good; Fair; Poor; Bad.

ISBN 0-8437-7970-5

PRINTED IN THE UNITED STATES OF AMERICA

LESSON 1

abdicate abrogate disseminate expiate fabricate gesticulate propitiate relegate ruminate vitiate

A Each of the following sentences contains a verb in **bold type** followed by three possible meanings. Circle the letter of the choice that comes closest to the meaning of the **bold** word. Check your answers in a dictionary.

B 1. When King Lear decided to **abdicate** his high office, he wanted to divide his kingdom among his daughters.
   a. deny b. relinquish c. abolish

A 2. When the kings became personally hostile to one another, they ordered their prime ministers to **abrogate** the mutual defense treaty.
   a. abolish b. relinquish c. deny

C 3. In ancient times, news was **disseminated** largely by word of mouth.
   a. gathered b. verified c. spread

B 4. The monk decided to **expiate** his sins by wearing a hair shirt.
   a. avoid b. atone for c. repress

A 5. He **fabricated** a story about a flat tire so that his parents would not punish him for staying out late.
   a. made up b. testified to c. rehearsed

B 6. She **gesticulated** wildly to signal her distress to her friend, who stood behind the monster's back.
   a. coughed b. gestured c. grunted

C 7. The savages tried to **propitiate** their gods' anger by burning a bull on the altar.
   a. lessen b. do away with c. appease

8. After Jackson had made three errors in one game, the coach **relegated** him to the junior varsity.
   a. demoted b. directed c. reversed

9. She wanted to **ruminate** over his proposal for a few days before deciding.
   a. talk about b. debate c. ponder

10. The professor complained that poor television dramas had **vitiated** the tastes of her students.
   a. changed b. vitalized c. debased

WORKING WITH WORDS:
The prefix **ab-**, which is used in **abdicate** and **abrogate**, means "away," "from," "away from," or "off." Can you combine this prefix with the following Latin roots to make five English verbs? Check your answers in a dictionary.

LATIN ROOT		ENGLISH VERB
ducere:	to lead	______________
horrere:	to shudder	______________
jurare:	to swear	______________

negare: to deny ____________________

solvere: to loose, free ____________________

B Write a form of one of the lesson words in Activity A in the blank space in each of the sentences below.

1. Since all the students are home on vacation, how shall we ______________ the information that school will open a day later than anticipated?

2. The air in the room was ______________ by the smelly gases.

3. It was determined that the agreement could be ______________ only by mutual consent of the nations that signed it.

4. We saw him standing in the middle of the highway as he ______________ furiously, hoping to stop a car.

5. Will it satisfy the victim if the criminal is sent to jail to ______________ his crime?

6. When the Duke married his cleaning lady, his subjects insisted that he ______________ his dukedom.

7. If you ______________ explanations all the time, no one will believe in you.

8. Philosophers are persons who like to ______________ over problems.

9. Her father was upset over the accident, and she was trying to figure out a way to ______________ him so that she could have the car again.

10. The President ______________ minor duties to his Vice-President to perform.

WORKING WITH WORDS:
Every verb in this lesson ends in the suffix **-ate**. Commonly, such verbs may be made into nouns ending in **-ation**. Make **-ation** nouns out of at least five verbs, and write a sentence for each in the blanks below.

1. ____
2. ____
3. ____
____
4. ____
____
5. ____
____

LESSON 2

egress ingress anomaly cataclysm equanimity hierarchy machination temerity travesty truism

A Each of the following sentences contains a noun in **bold type**. Try to determine the meaning of the noun from the context; then write a possible meaning in the space provided. Check your answers in a dictionary.

1. When the wall caved in, there was no longer any **egress** ___exit___ from the place in which the miners were working.
2. Nor could the rescue workers find any **ingress** ___entrance___ through which they might go to save them.
3. The newly discovered phenomenon did not fit into any known scientific laws, so that the scientists classified it as an **anomaly** ___abnormality___
4. The earthquake produced such a **cataclysm** ___disaster___ that it was doubtful that the island would ever be the same again.
5. Mrs. Friend has lived a productive and happy life, and she now faces her final years with the **equanimity** ___serenity___ of one who has nothing to fear.
6. "A deck of cards was built like the purest of **hierarchies** ___structured social system___ with every card a master to those below it." (Culbertson)
7. Mary Queen of Scots was involved in **machinations** ___conspiracy___ against her cousin, Queen Elizabeth.
8. No one had the **temerity** ___audacity___ to talk back to the Empress; to do so might cost one's head.
9. The young writer produced a **travesty** ___disaster___ when he tried to make Tolstoy's "War and Peace" into a three-act play.
10. That men need women, and women, men is a **truism** ___truth___.

WORKING WITH WORDS:
Egress and **ingress** are so close in form that you may have difficulty telling which means which. Try to keep them straight by remembering that the **in-** of **ingress** means "in" or "into." An **ingress** is a going in or a means or place of going in; it may also mean the right or permission to enter. **Egress** refers to a going out or a means or place of going out; it may refer to the right of going out. Write the proper word of this pair in the blanks in the sentences below.

1. The guard denied the peasants ___ingress___ to the palace.
2. Every theater must have more than one ___egress___ through which patrons may escape in case of fire.
3. We could find no ___egress___ from the Hall of Mirrors.
4. The hero could not save the heroine, for he could find no ___ingress___ to the fiend's castle where she was being held captive.

B Write a form of one of the lesson words in Activity A in the blank space in each of the sentences below.

1. The students acted so badly that they made a/an ~~catastrophe~~ travesty of "Hamlet."
2. A person without fingerprints would be a/an anomaly.
3. The Princess was not granted egress from the castle grounds unattended until she was eighteen years old.
4. One's values are always arranged in a/an hierarchy, as one soon discovers when two primary values conflict and one must choose one or the other.
5. A writer who states only truisms is not likely to engage his readers' attention.
6. The King learned of the machinations of his Prime Minister and put him to death forthwith.
7. Have you the temerity to enter a boxing ring with the Golden Gloves champion?
8. Personally, I hope you can't find ingress to the boxing arena.
9. Don is noted for his equanimity of temper; thus we were glad to have him with us when the crisis occurred.
10. The revolution produced a/an cataclysm, which threatened the structure of the society.

WORKING WITH WORDS:
Below is a group of eighteen words followed by six words from this lesson. Choose for each of the six words three synonyms from the group of eighteen. Write these words in the appropriate blanks below. Check your answers in a dictionary, and if your teacher asks, also check on the precise meaning of each of the synonyms.

effrontery ✓	caricature	serenity ✓
composure ✓	platitude	impetuosity ✓
parody ✓	cabal ✓	conspiracy ✓
holocaust ✓	bromide	banality ✓
collusion ✓	debacle	calamity ✓
nonchalance ✓	audacity ✓	lampoon ✓

1. cataclysm	holocaust	calamity	debacle
2. equanimity	composure	nonchalance	serenity
3. machination	conspiracy	cabal	collusion
4. temerity	audacity	effrontary	impetuosity
5. travesty	lampoon	parody	~~banality~~ caricature
6. truism	~~audacity~~		

LESSON 3

carnivorous centrifugal decadent defunct inane incipient incoherent moot perfidious posthumous

A Each of the following sentences contains an adjective in **bold type**. Study each sentence carefully to determine the meaning of the word. Below the sentences are ten definitions. Choose the definition that goes with each **bold** word. In the space before each definition write the number of the sentence in which the word it defines appears. Check your answers in a dictionary.

1. Many **carnivorous** predators, such as wolves, choose smaller, herbivorous animals, such as rabbits, as their prey.
2. The car took the turn at such a high speed that the **centrifugal** force threw me against the door.
3. Growing slums and increases in pollution indicate that our cities are **decadent**.
4. From the boarded up doors and windows, we assumed that the little restaurant had become **defunct**.
5. Much cocktail party talk is altogether **inane**; cocktail parties are not the place for serious conversations.
6. The **incipient** cloudiness on the horizon should have warned us of the coming storm.
7. The dying woman tried to speak, but could only manage an **incoherent** mumble.
8. The point was **moot**, but since no one wished to argue it, it was allowed to go unchallenged.
9. Having once betrayed his best friend, Charles was considered too **perfidious** to be worthy of trust.
10. Some claimed that his **posthumous** poems were better than those he had published while he was alive.

A. __7__ disjointed
B. __4__ dead
C. __8__ arguable
D. __1__ meat-eating
E. __9__ treacherous
F. __5__ lacking substance or sense
G. __6__ just beginning to appear
H. __3__ declining, decaying
I. __2__ away from the center
J. __10__ issued after death

WORKING WITH WORDS:
It is often good to learn words in sets. For example, while learning the meaning of **carnivorous**, one should also add **herbivorous** and **omnivorous** to his vocabulary. Similarly, it is economical to learn the meaning of **centripetal** at the same time that one learns **centrifugal**. Be sure you know the meaning of all five of these words; then write the proper word in each of the blank spaces below.

1. One would assume that a/an __omnivorous__ animal would have a better chance of survival than one whose eating habits were more narrow.
2. Most farm animals, such as the cow, are essentially __herbivorous__
3. At parties, Susan was so attractive that we nicknamed her the __centripetal__ force.

B Write a form of one of the lesson words in Activity A in the blank space in each of the sentences below.

1. The fireman who died while rescuing children from the nursery home was given two _posthumous_ citations for bravery.
2. He knew that he had to slow the train down somehow, or the _centrifugal_ pull on the next turn would derail it.
3. After he himself had lost the nomination, Hector became a/an _perfidious_ plotter against the party's nominee.
4. Whether or not Doris had committed the crime was a/an _moot_ question, until the eyewitness testified.
5. When they are in a/an _incipient_ stage, one can't tell a chicken from an eagle.
6. The strike lasted so long that the newspaper became _defunct_ and everyone was out of a job.
7. After winning the million-dollar lottery, Mrs. Watson was too _incoherent_ with joy to speak to the reporters.
8. I thought the film was _inane_, until the movie critic convinced me of its substance.
9. When she discovered that the whole art exhibit consisted of black squares, she decided that the state of contemporary art was _inane_ decaying
10. We thought our cat wasn't truly _carnivorous_ until we saw how much it relished eating the mouse.

WORKING WITH WORDS:
Several of the adjectives in this lesson have related nouns. Some of the nouns are spelled like the adjectives, but others may be used as nouns with only a change of spelling. Write nouns in the blank spaces below, making sure that each of them is the same as or is related to an adjective in this lesson.

1. The writer was called a/an _decadent_ because she sought inspiration in the neurotic and morbid.
2. Can you tell me whether or not a deer is a/an _carnivore_?
3. The teacher gave a low grade to the essay because of its _incoherence_.
4. In ancient times English freemen of a shire could hold a/an _moot_ to discuss what they should do about the threat of war.
5. A leader who violates the trust of the voters is guilty of _perfidy_.

Review 1

A In each group underline the word or expression which has a similar meaning to the first (**bold**) word.

anomaly: anonymity, disbelief, irregularity, eccentricity
egress: exit, increase, decrease, entrance
carnivorous: carnival-like, flesh-eating, hungry, attractive
gesticulate: motion vigorously, deliver orally, deceive, establish
abrogate: alter, cancel, confirm, demand
incoherent: unconnected, unconscious, unlikely, included
defunct: desperate, degraded, dead, substituted
equanimity: equality, composure, horsemanship, unusualness
truism: frankness, cliché, dullness, absolute
fabricate: finish, multiply, frequent, forge
travesty: travel, mockery, treachery, falsification
hierarchy: kingdom, ranking, rule by decree, value
posthumous: afterdeath, afterlife, ultimate, unsigned
centrifugal: powerful, frugal, away from the center, toward the center
propitiate: thank, appease, worship, pity
decadent: decayed, clumsy, restless, excitable
vitiate: venerate, vitalize, visit, corrupt
ingress: go forward, transgress, right to enter, start up
disseminate: weaken, destroy completely, dissolve, distribute
incipient: initial, obvious, unsightly, unconscious

B Choose suitable words from the list given below, and fill in the blanks. You may have to alter some of the words.

When his advisers warned the stupid dictator about the ________________ of some of his ________________ subjects, he replied with ________________ comments on his popularity and said that nobody would have the ________________ to challenge his sovereignty. When the ________________ finally erupted, the dictator was forced to ________________. What to do with their former master was a ________________ question among the insurgents. It was finally decided to ________________ him to a prison on a barren isle, where he could ________________ his crimes and ________________ on his evil life.

relegate	**perfidious**	**temerity**	**inane**	**machination**
cataclysm	**ruminate**	**abdicate**	**moot**	**expiate**

C Replace each word or expression in **bold type** by a word from Lesson 1, 2, or 3.

1. If you cannot tell the truth, **make up a story**.
2. The **afterdeath** award consoled the widow of the policeman.
3. All commoners were refused **the permission to enter**.
4. She **made deliberate motions** to the other drivers to warn them that there was an accident ahead.
5. There remained one **deviation from the normal** for which he could not account.
6. The play was a **grotesque imitation** of life in the twenties.
7. He bores me because he keeps mouthing **self-evident statements**.
8. When she tried to describe the accident, she became **unable to express her thoughts in an orderly manner**.
9. He was urged to **make atonement for** his sins before it was too late.
10. Her **quality of being even-tempered** makes her easy to get along with.
11. There is a distinct **organization according to rank** in the military.
12. For homework, we had to **ponder deeply** upon the questions raised in class
13. That all men are entitled to equal justice is not an **arguable** proposition.
14. The boy showed **contempt of danger** by standing up to the gang.
15. I never thought my best friend would be so **basely false to trust**.

D Match up each word in Column A with a suitable word in Column B. Write the word from Column B in its correct place beside the word in Column A.

A		B
abrogate	________	organization
centrifugal	________	the wrath of the gods
defunct	________	from the theater
egress	________	an agreement
inane	________	motion
propitiate	________	remarks

E Find in Lesson 1, 2, or 3 a word which is derived from each of the following roots. Write it in the space provided.

cadere (L) — fall ________ dicare (L) — proclaim ________

machina (Gk) — contrivance ________ incipere (L) — begin ________

seminare (L) — sow ________ vitium (L) — evil ________

klyzein (Gk) — wash ________ legare (L) — leave ________

vorare (L) — swallow ________

LESSON 4

abet abridge alleviate disparage elucidate eschew expedite petrify reverberate satiate

elucidate

A Each of the following sentences contains a verb in **bold type**. Try to determine the meaning of the verb from the context; then write a possible meaning in the space provided. Check your answers in a dictionary.

1. The gambler planned the robbery, but he needed a good safecracker to **abet** ___aid___ him.
2. The chairman told him to **abridge** ___shorten___ his speech, because the audience was falling asleep.
3. He might also **alleviate** ___stop___ their suffering simply by stopping his speech now.
4. The sprinter **disparaged** ___belittled___ women's athletic achievements by pointing out that he could run the 100-yard dash faster than any woman in the world.
5. Mr. Jordan is an excellent teacher; he can **elucidate** ___explain___ even very obscure and complex ideas, such as the theory of relativity.
6. Aristotle claimed that a wise man would **eschew** ___avoid___ extremes, preferring the "golden mean" in conduct.
7. Mona's new plan helped to **expedite** ___speed up___ official business; what used to require five hours of work now requires only one.
8. Snakes **petrified** ___scared___ him to such an extent that he refused even to go for a walk in the woods.
9. The sound of their voices **reverberated** ___echoed___ throughout the cave, but we could not discover where it was coming from.
10. The Romans drank and ate until they were **satiated** ___fully satisfied___; then they spent days recovering from their gluttony.

WORKING WITH WORDS:
Verb forms with past (usually **-ed**) and present (**-ing**) participial endings may often be placed before nouns in order to modify them. For example, we may speak of an abridg**ed** dictionary or an elucidat**ing** remark. Try your own hand at creating similar phrases with other words from this lesson. Write your phrases in the blank spaces.

PRESENT PARTICIPLES	PAST PARTICIPLES
______________	______________
______________	______________
______________	______________

B Write a form of one of the lesson words in Activity A in the blank space in each of the sentences below.

1. The thought of getting lost in the fun house *petrified* her, and she stood at the entrance, unable to move.
2. I was *satiated* by the Thanksgiving dinner and didn't want to eat again for days.
3. The scholar was asked to *abridge* his article so that it could be included in a list of abstracts.
4. John constantly *disparaged* his younger brother's report cards, but he didn't have all A's when he was in fifth grade.
5. Man must learn to *eschew* violence, or we will never have a peaceful world.
6. There is too much red tape around here; we must devise a way to *expedite* our work.
7. At the conclusion of the concert, applause *reverberated* throughout the hall.
8. Although we cannot solve the poverty problem, there are many things we can do to *alleviate* the misery of poor families.
9. One doesn't have to commit a crime to go to jail; to *abet* a criminal is also a punishable offense.
10. Someone from the audience asked the speaker to *elucidate* one of his more obscure remarks.

WORKING WITH WORDS:
Below is a group of eighteen words followed by six words from this lesson. Choose for each of the six words three synonyms from the group of eighteen. Write these words in the appropriate blanks below. Check your answers in a dictionary, and if your teacher asks, also check on the precise meaning of each of the synonyms.

1 foment	6 belittle	3 evade
5 assuage	6 decry	1 facilitate
4 accelerate	construe	1 incite
5 allay	3 shun	5 mitigate
3 elude	4 precipitate	2 expound
instigate	2 explicate	6 censure

1. abet ________ ________ ________
2. elucidate ________ ________ ________
3. eschew ________ ________ ________
4. expedite ________ ________ ________
5. alleviate ________ ________ ________
6. disparage ________ ________ ________

LESSON 5

etymology alacrity autonomy calumny felicity innuendo paragon pedant unanimity veracity

VERACITY

A Each of the following sentences contains a noun in **bold type**. Study each sentence carefully to determine the meaning of the word. Below the sentences are ten definitions. Choose the definition that goes with each **bold** word. In the space before each definition, write the number of the sentence in which the word it defines appears. Check your answers in a dictionary.

1. The **etymology** of a given word may be checked in a good dictionary; you may find that the word is Latin or Greek in origin.
2. Impressed with the **alacrity** with which the worker carried out orders, the plant manager promoted him to foreman.
3. Over the past several decades many African nations have gained **autonomy** and are no longer tied to Europe's apron strings.
4. She accused him of **calumny** when he testified that the accident was her responsibility; he knew she was not at fault.
5. Marsha has always been a happy person, but she has never known such **felicity** as she is experiencing in her marriage to Jim.
6. He said that he had never seen me thinner, but I caught the **innuendo** in his remark suggesting that I was still too fat.
7. It is hard to believe that she is the **paragon** of virtue that she is said to be.
8. Fred is such a **pedant** — he knows everything from books and shows it off, but he knows nothing of practical affairs.
9. I have never seen such **unanimity** in our State Senate as I did on the day they passed a bill raising their own salaries.
10. There was no question about the **veracity** of his reports; everything that he said was checked and verified.

A. __2__ swiftness

B. __6__ hint

C. __3__ self-government

D. __7__ perfect example

E. __5__ great happiness

F. __1__ origin and history

G. __10__ truth, honesty

H. __9__ complete agreement

I. __8__ person who displays learning

J. __4__ malicious falsehood

WORKING WITH WORDS:
When a word ends in **-ology**, it usually refers to the study of something. **Etymology** refers to the study of "etymons" or the ancestors, so to speak, of words. Can you define the "**-ology** words" below? Write the definition in the blank spaces, using a dictionary, if necessary.

1. anthropology: the study of __man__
2. entomology: the study of __insects__
3. ethnology: the study of __culture__
4. ornithology: the study of __birds__
5. paleontology: the study of __prehistoric bones__

B Write a form of one of the lesson words in Activity A in the blank space in each of the sentences below.

1. Her handwriting is a/an paragon of excellence; she forms every letter with extreme care.
2. Many teenagers have to struggle for autonomy against the wishes of possessive parents.
3. He's such a/an pedant; he can't even talk about the weather without referring to a book he has read.
4. Ken runs with the swiftness of molasses, but his mind moves with the alacrity of that of a genius.
5. Her reputation is so spotless that she can put down any calumny.
6. If you want ~~etymology~~ unanimity of opinion from the students, ask them if they would like to extend the Christmas vacation for a week.
7. George Washington was a model of veracity.
8. The word's etymology indicates that it is from the Greek.
9. It's not the calumnies voiced about his income taxes that bother Senator X but the whispered innuendo about him and his wife.
10. A jug of wine, a book of verse, and a girl beside him added up to felicity for Omar Khayyām.

WORKING WITH WORDS:
Observe that many of the nouns in this lesson share the same ending. Such nouns typically may be made into adjectives by taking on another suffix. Can you determine what this suffix is and write five sentences of your own using the adjective form? Write your sentences in the blank spaces below.

1. ____________________

2. ____________________

3. ____________________

____

4. ____________________

____

5. ____________________

____

LESSON 6

succinct taciturn cogent cognizant commensurate ebullient mandatory rapacious reprehensible sporadic

taciturn

A Each of the following sentences contains an adjective in **bold type** followed by three possible meanings. Circle the letter of the choice that comes closest to the meaning of the **bold** word. Check your answers in a dictionary.

1. His answer was quite **succinct**: "Scram!"
   a. harsh b. instantaneous c. concise, clear

2. Hilda is so **taciturn** in her dealings with people that you might think each word she spoke cost her money.
   a. ill-mannered b. sparing with speech c. deadly

3. The reasons the salesman gave for buying a lightning rod were so **cogent** that he sold one to everybody in town.
   a. persuasive b. complex c. realistic

4. A student who wishes to go to college should be **cognizant** of college admission policies.
   a. careful b. aware c. considerate

5. The value of my grandmother's ring, which was $40, was certainly not **commensurate** with my high expectations.
   a. proportionate b. measurable c. comfortable

6. The children were so **ebullient** on Christmas Eve that we thought they would not be able to get to sleep.
   a. hopeful b. extraordinary c. overflowing with excitement

7. It is **mandatory** for students who wish to earn a doctor's degree from this school to be able to read two foreign languages.
   a. expected b. required c. manageable

8. A **rapacious** horde of locusts descended on the field and stripped it bare.
   a. overwhelming b. greedy c. ridiculous

9. Beating up an old woman is the most **reprehensible** act I know.
   a. blameworthy b. impulsive c. pointless

10. He worked at the task in a rather **sporadic** manner, stopping every now and then for a cigarette or a cup of coffee.
    a. sleepy b. irregular c. spontaneous

WORKING WITH WORDS:
In some dictionaries, you will find **laconic** listed as a synonym for both **succinct** and **taciturn**. Yet there is certainly a difference in meaning between these two words. To prove you know the difference, write six of the words below in the blank spaces next to **succinct** and the other six next to **taciturn**.

silent	terse	epigrammatic	uncommunicative	summary	secretive
concise	pithy	tightlipped	compendious	reserved	reticent

1. succinct ________ ________ ________ ________ ________ ________

2. taciturn ________ ________ ________ ________ ________ ________

Look up the meaning and origin of **laconic** and be prepared to discuss why it may be used as a synonym for both **succinct** and **taciturn**.

B Write a form of one of the lesson words in Activity A in the blank space in each of the sentences below.

1. Portia convinced the officer that her speeding was not reprehensible: she was a volunteer fire person going to a fire.
2. It was mandatory to pay dues before being allowed voting privileges.
3. Among the most ________________ statements on modern art is "Less is more."
4. Miles offered several reasons for voting for his candidate, but none was cogent enough to convince me to do the same.
5. Her interest in men was ________________, and she never married.
6. The New Year's Eve party was quite ebullient for a time, but the excitement waned after midnight.
7. He is much too taciturn to become a good lawyer.
8. I told the officer that I was not ________________ of the fact that I was in a speed zone, but he wasn't impressed by my excuse.
9. The energy he spent campaigning was not ________________ with his third-place finish.
10. Her hunger for knowledge was so ________________ that she read the encyclopedia from cover to cover.

WORKING WITH WORDS:
Choose from the list below the adjective which fits best in the blank space in each of the phrases that follow.

sporadic, cogent, cognizant, ebullient, mandatory, rapacious, reprehensible, carnivorous, incoherent

1. a/an ________________ rule
2. a/an ________________ argument
3. a/an ________________ appetite
4. a/an ________________ crime
5. a/an ________________ personality
6. ________________ of the conditions

Review 2

Write one of the words listed above each set of paragraphs in the blank spaces below. You might have to alter the form of some of the nouns by making them plural or some of the verbs by making them past tense.

etymology
felicity
mandatory
satiate
cognizant
reverberate
commensurate
unanimity
paragon
pedant

We would probably find a near (1) *unanimity* among readers of poetry for the claim that the reputation of the English Romantic poets is (2) *commensurate* with that of any other group of poets. Though the Romantics wrote a century and a half ago, their words have (3) *reverbrated* in the minds of English-speaking people ever since. Their works never (4) *satiate* us; they have never ceased to bring (5) *felicity* to lovers of poetry. Reading them has become (6) *mandatory* for anyone who wishes to be considered educated.

If you are (7) *cognizant* of the (8) *etymology* of the word "romance," you know that it originally meant a vernacular descended from the Latin; then it came to mean the literature written in the vernacular, and finally it meant the prevailing kind of literature. One need not be a/an (9) *pedant* to know that the first romances were long tales of the adventures of chivalric heroes enamored of ladies who were (10) *paragons* of virtue.

alleviate
eschew
alacrity
succinct
elucidate
taciturn
disparage
cogent
abet
veracity

Wordsworth, Coleridge, Keats, Shelley, and Byron — to name the best known Romantic poets — did not altogether (11)________________ this type of romance; but many of their most famous poems were not long tales at all but (12) ________________ lyrics. One of the best of English Romantic poems, for example, is Keats' "La Belle Dame Sans Merci," which is only forty-eight lines long. It is about a lonely, (13) *taciturn* lover, who cannot (14) *elucidate* the pain he feels as a result of a hopeless love. Some critics have sought to (15) elucidate this poem by reference to Keats' own hopeless love for Fanny Brawne, and they have presented (16) cogent arguments on behalf of their explanation. Although we do not wish to (17) abet this theory, it is true that Keats' despair was certainly at least (18) [illegible] by the (19)________________ with which his symptoms of tuberculosis were spreading. In any event, the poem is memorable for the (20) veracity of its expression of a state of wretchedness.

abridge
petrify
autonomy
sporadic
reprehensible
ebullient
rapacious
innuendo
expiate
calumny

Critics — especially critics who were also poets — have not always been as fond of the Romantics as have readers, and there have been (21) sporadic attacks against Romantic poetry in our own time by (22)________________ poet-critics — or should we call them vultures? Often, these critics have been seeking to prove their own (23)________________; sometimes, indeed, they may have felt a need to (24)________________ a tendency to copy the Romantics. While such critics have rarely been so (25)________________ as to spread (26)________________ about their poet ancestors, one commonly finds a/an (27)________________ that the Romantics were not as good as the moderns. The most common criticism is that the Romantics were too (28)________________ and consequently were careless of their techniques.

We must (29)________________ this discussion, and thus we cannot further discuss the merits and defects of the arguments of some defenders of modern poetry against Romantic poetry. But we will note, in conclusion, that a healthy impulse behind such criticism is that good poets do not want to (30)________________ poetic traditions. It was this same impulse, in part, that led the Romantics to criticize the eighteenth-century poets who preceded them.

LESSON 7

collaborate accede connive culminate exude galvanize infringe append jeopardize sully

GALVANIZE

A Each of the following sentences contains a verb in **bold type**. Study each sentence carefully to determine the meaning of the word. Below the sentences are ten definitions. Choose the definition that goes with each **bold** word. In the space before each definition, .vrite the number of the sentence in which the word it defines appears. Check your answers in a dictionary.

1. The mayor **collaborated** with the enemy to the extent of providing food and shelter, but he refused to help them in any other way.
2. He **acceded** to their request for basic needs, but housed them in a barn and fed them oats.
3. The watchman **connived** with the burglars to plot the perfect crime.
4. Her education finally **culminated** in a doctor's degree.
5. She **exudes** charm the way an athlete pours off sweat.
6. In electric shock therapy, a patient is **galvanized** as he lies strapped to a table.
7. We believe in freedom of action, but we also believe that one must not **infringe** on the rights of others.
8. Students must **append** to the body of their reports a bibliography of their readings.
9. A student who cheats on an examination **jeopardizes** his class standing, for if he is caught, he gets a zero for the course.
10. George was not concerned with getting a lower grade; he did not cheat because he did not want to **sully** his good reputation.

A. __9__ endanger

B. __3__ cooperate secretly

C. __1__ work jointly with

D. __5__ discharge

E. __7__ trespass

F. __2__ consent

G. __8__ attach

H. __10__ soil, tarnish

I. __6__ stimulate, electrify

J. __4__ reach a highest point

WORKING WITH WORDS:
Notice the word **labor** in col**labor**ate. The word means "to work (labor) together." Be sure that you can distinguish this word from another that sounds and looks something like it — **corroborate** **Corroborate** means "to lend support to" or "to attest the truth or accuracy of." Remember this sentence:

Although the scientists often **collaborated**, they did not always **corroborate** one another's research findings.

Use, and spell correctly, the proper one of this confusing pair in the blanks below:

1. The eyewitness __corroborated__ the testimony of the driver.
2. You can't expect me to __corroborate__ that phony story of yours.

3. The car salesman asked the writer to collaborate with him in writing a book on how to buy used cars.

4. The vice-leader of the gang was secretly collaborate ing with the FBI.

B Write a form of one of the lesson words in Activity A in the blank space in each of the sentences below.

1. The truant officer knew that cutting school was illegal, yet he acceded to the students' breaking the law on their birthdays.

2. One who climbs rocks on a rainy day jeopardizes his life.

3. The day-long Fourth of July celebration culminate in a massive display of fireworks.

4. Students are encouraged to collaborate with one another in the chemistry laboratory.

5. A type of sugar may be made from the sap that exudes from maple trees.

6. An unscrupulous newspaper editor tried to sully the good name of the candidate by publishing innuendoes which were very detrimental to his character.

7. Though mothers are generally placid, they may be galvanized into action by any threat to their young.

8. A mother bear will attack anyone who infringes upon her home territory.

9. When King Henry died, the Prince ________ his father to the crown.

10. Vocabulary notes were appended to each chapter of the textbook.

WORKING WITH WORDS:
Write the verb from this lesson that commonly works with the word or words listed below. Although the verb may not always work with the listed word, it is generally a good idea to memorize these little words along with the meaning of the verb.

1. ________ to
2. ________ at, with
3. ________ with
4. ________ in
5. ________ into
6. ________ on, upon
7. ________ from

LESSON 8

epicure nemesis antithesis avocation bureaucracy disparity increment kleptomaniac oligarchy topography

KL PTO- MANI C

A Each of the following sentences contains a noun in **bold type** followed by three possible meanings. Circle the letter of the choice that comes closest to the meaning of the **bold** word. Check your answers in a dictionary.

1. The **epicure** would not eat at the new restaurant because the food and wine were not of the best quality.
   a. restaurant owner b. Frenchman c. person particular about food
2. Our football team had won every game until it met its **nemesis**.
   a. formidable rival b. substitute team c. traditional rival
3. In many ways, communism is the **antithesis** of democracy.
   a. greatest threat b. descendant c. direct opposite
4. Mr. Thomas is a lawyer by profession; his **avocation** is stamp collecting.
   a. specialty b. hobby c. enthusiasm
5. There are so many departments in our government that it may be accurate to say that we are ruled by a **bureaucracy**.
   a. chief executive b. semiofficial body c. group of nonelected officials
6. There was quite a **disparity** between his pledge to give a thousand dollars and the hundred dollars he actually gave.
   a. difference b. large amount c. dishonesty
7. All the workers wanted was an **increment** in their salaries to keep up with the cost of living.
   a. fringe benefit b. difference c. increase
8. The judge decided to send the **kleptomaniac** to a mental institution rather than to prison.
   a. criminal b. delinquent c. obsessive thief
9. So strong were the members of the President's Cabinet that that part of the government was actually run by an **oligarchy** rather than one man.
   a. small controlling group b. legislative body c. nonpolitical system
10. The **topography** of Korea was such that it was easy to fight a conventional type of war there.
   a. government b. physical features c. military system

WORKING WITH WORDS:
Many of our words were originally the names of persons, gods or goddesses, or places of ancient Greece. Check the etymology of two such words from this lesson in your dictionary — **epicure** and **nemesis**. Then use your dictionary to discover the meaning and origin of the following words. Write the information in the blank spaces.

1. atlas ____________________
2. marathon ____________________

3. sybarite ______________________________

4. thespian ______________________________

5. tyrant ______________________________

B Write a form of one of the lesson words in Activity A in the blank space in each of the sentences below.

1. After he had retired, he was able to spend all of his time on his avocation, which was the collection of model trains.
2. The pay increment that he received was eaten up entirely by taxes.
3. The main requirement the epicure was looking for in a wife was that she be a good cook.
4. We studied the topography carefully to determine whether we could reach our destination by jeep.
5. Steve was the antithesis of what Sharon was looking for in a man—short, fat, and ugly.
6. Athens was governed for some time by a/an oligarchy of superior men.
7. The kleptomaniac preferred to do his "business" in the larger department stores.
8. The survey revealed that there was a considerable disparity between the salaries of males and females on the college faculty.
9. There was such a powerful and extensive governmental bureaucracy that no one could get to see the head of the agency.
10. John acted as a kind of self-appointed nemesis to avenge the wrongs his family had suffered.

WORKING WITH WORDS:
Use each prefix below at least twice, combining it with the stems on the right to make words. Write the eight words you make in the third column and after this write a definition of each word.

PREFIX	STEM	WORD	DEFINITION
auto-	archy	____________	______________________
demo-	cracy	____________	______________________
mon/mono-	graphy	____________	______________________
pyro-	maniac	____________	______________________
		____________	______________________
		____________	______________________
		____________	______________________
		____________	______________________

LESSON 9

blatant adroit altruistic benign chronological contentious crass evasive gratuitous punctilious

evasive

A Each of the following sentences contains an adjective in **bold type**. Try to determine the meaning of the adjective from the context; then write a possible meaning in the space provided. Check your answers in a dictionary.

1. He kept talking on and on, in **blatant** obvious disregard of the wishes of others who wanted to express themselves.

2. Manuel was so **adroit** dextrous as a woodsman that we were pleased to have him with us on our trip into the wilderness.

3. One rarely meets today the kind of **altruistic** helpful behavior shown by the Good Samaritan — except perhaps at Christmastime.

4. Animals seemed to sense her **benign** kind nature and would naturally approach her to be fed or petted.

5. In the test we had to put the battles in **chronological** time sequence order, from the earliest to the latest.

6. He has such a **contentious** argumentative disposition that we think he might be a good lawyer, as long as he can keep from antagonizing jurors.

7. It was the kind of **crass** crude joke that was all right for an audience of poker-playing cronies but out of place at a cocktail party.

8. I was hoping for a straight "yes" or "no," but instead she gave me an **evasive** avoiding answer.

9. No one cared about or asked for it, but Sheila gave her **gratuitous** free criticism anyway.

10. He was normally so **punctilious** extremely proper that everyone was shocked when he started to eat his pudding with a knife.

WORKING WITH WORDS:
In choosing words it is important to be aware of the principles of good usage. A case in point is the difference between **blatant** and **flagrant**. **Flagrant** stresses the extreme or deliberate nature of a wrong or an evil. **Blatant**, in contrast, refers to something unpleasantly loud or noisy or to something blundering or obvious. Both words might be used to modify a word like **lie**. But a **flagrant** lie would be shocking or morally repulsive, whereas a **blatant** lie would be an obvious or a blundering lie. Below are three more pairs of words that present usage problems. Look them up in a dictionary and write what information you discover in the blank spaces.

1. Anxious/eager: ____________________

____

2. Complete/finalize: ____________________

____

3. Fewer/less: ____

____

B Write a form of one of the lesson words in Activity A in the blank space in each of the sentences below.

1. Her motive for giving blood to the Red Cross was purely altruistic; she asked for neither praise nor payment.
2. Each Sunday the twelve children walked down the street in chronological order; the youngest walked last with his father.
3. It was a/an flatant error on the part of the shortstop to throw the ball to first base when he could have made a double play.
4. The crass behavior of the frontiersman was frowned upon by the members of Boston society.
5. The Christian missionary was a/an altruistic person, who selflessly tried to save souls.
6. My father's adroit driving through the snowstorm saved all our lives.
7. Politicians are usually skillful at giving evasive answers to questions.
8. There was quite a contrast between the twins—the one was as sloppy as the other was punctilions.
9. Santa Claus is a jolly and benign figure, but he has his origins in a forbidding fourth-century saint who was a stern judge of children's behavior.
10. Several rather contentious members of the audience kept interrupting the speaker to take issue with his arguments.

WORKING WITH WORDS:
A synonym does not mean precisely the same thing as another word. Study the sentences below and choose and circle the word that seems to **best** express the meaning intended by the sentence.

1. To be a good pianist, one needs (adroit, deft, nimble) hands.
2. Tom was such a (punctilious, fastidious, conscientious) worker that he never took a day off unless he was really sick.
3. Our Secretary of State claimed that the (contentious, belligerent, pugnacious) nations would soon end their war.
4. The (crass, indelicate, ribald) comedian used off-color language to get laughs from his audience.
5. He purposely gave (evasive, abstruse, ambiguous) answers because he wanted to dodge the political issues involved in the questions.
6. A (benign, compassionate, gracious) nature is one easily moved to sympathy or pity.

Review 3

A In each group underline the word or expression which has a similar meaning to the first (**bold**) word.

accede: make real, praise, demand, consent
crass: dull witted, shameful, gross, miserly
increment: release, salary, increase, subtraction
sully: make foolish, dirty, insult, stimulate
punctilious: fearful, punctual, precise, proud
contentious: quarrelsome, conscientious, cowardly, cautious
kleptomaniac: careful person, deceiver, compulsive thief, one who kills
infringe: violate rights, embroider, surround, disturb order
epicure: grocer, lover of spices, fat person, lover of good food
exude: swell up, boast, discharge, dig up
antithesis: double meaning, opposite, antipathy, act of a play
connive: deceive, cooperate secretly, convince, abolish
gratuitous: foolish, effective, elaborate, given freely
collaborate: copy, have pity for, work jointly, verify
altruistic: selfless, completely true, self-governing, foolish
topography: a type of writing, configuration, episode, art of analysis
blatant: brutal, obtrusive, stupid, brazen
avocation: vocation, legal status, assertion, hobby
evasive: fleeting, eager, unfrank, invading
append: add on, abridge, appeal to, advance

B Choose suitable words from the list given below, and fill in the blanks.

In ____________ terms, Athens is often considered the first democracy; yet it was really a type of ____________, because only about 10 percent of the people actually voted. Another ____________ between them and us is that they had no ____________ to speak of, for their officeholders were chosen by lot and offices rotated. Athenian power and culture ____________ed in the Golden Age of Pericles. Pericles was a/an ____________ statesman, and his leadership had a particularly ____________ influence on the arts. However, near the end of his period of leadership, he ____________ed all he had accomplished in a war with Athens' old ____________, Sparta. It was his speech to the Athenian assembly that ____________ed the latter into action and promoted what is known as the Peloponnesian War.

chronological	**galvanize**	**adroit**	**disparity**	**benign**
bureaucracy	**oligarchy**	**nemesis**	**jeopardize**	**culminate**

C Replace each word or expression in **bold type** by a word from Lesson 7, 8, or 9, altering them if necessary.

1. Jack's **vulgarly noisy** behavior has alienated many of his friends.
2. The real cowboy tended to be more **coarse and unrefined** than his Hollywood image.
3. My **chief interest outside of work or profession** is the study of shells.
4. Dr. Franklin was an unusually **attentive to details** scientist.
5. I hate politicians who are **not straightforward**.
6. The party **reached its highest point** when the band marched into the room.
7. Maybe he'd occasionally win an argument if his manner were less **naturally disputatious**.
8. Her temperament is the **direct opposite** of mine.
9. School principals today are much more **kind and gentle** than they used to be.
10. Nurses are known for their **regard for others** nature.
11. The **skillful** skiier descended the steep slope without injury.
12. The flyer was familiar with the **shape of the surfaces** below him.
13. My **raises in pay** have not kept up with the cost of living.
14. The act of war **endangered** the new peace treaty.
15. The **person particular about his tastes** opened his own restaurant.

D Match up each word in Column A with a suitable word or expression in Column B.

A	B
accede ______	between the prices
sully ______	of the hero
nemesis ______	a note
galvanize ______	a reputation
append ______	to the request
disparity ______	our workers

E Find in Lesson 7, 8, or 9 a word which is derived from each of the following roots. Write it in the space provided.

connivere (L) — wink ______

oligos (Gk) — few ______

bureau (F) — office ______

sudare (L) — sweat ______

droit (F) — right ______

chronos (Gk) — time ______

kleptes (Gk) — thief ______

frangere (L) — break ______

gratia (L) — favor ______

LESSON 10 **abjure adjure commiserate correlate deplete defame disillusion dissemble domesticate stabilize**

deplete

A Each of the following sentences contains a verb in **bold type** followed by three possible meanings. Circle the letter of the choice that comes closest to the meaning of the **bold** word. Check your answers in a dictionary.

1. After the life of her child was saved by an operation, Mrs. Watson **abjured** all her previous opinions on the uselessness of medical science.
   a. renounced b. maintained c. absolved

2. The judge **adjured** the jury in the name of justice to consider the evidence with the greatest care.
   a. required b. charged solemnly c. instructed

3. Why do we **commiserate** with the poor only at Christmas and ignore them the rest of the year?
   a. complain over b. share c. pity

4. This year, we will **correlate** the study of American history with the study of American literature.
   a. correct b. consider carefully c. connect systematically

5. We cannot sell you any gas because the extra-heavy demands have **depleted** our supply.
   a. exhausted b. reduced c. destroyed

6. The politician claimed that his opponent was trying to **defame** him by suggesting that he had cheated on his income taxes.
   a. damage b. retaliate against c. dishonor

7. Thinking he was Napoleon made the patient so happy that the doctor tried not to **disillusion** him.
   a. dismay b. disenchant c. deceive

8. Susan tried to **dissemble** her true feelings for Harold by playing hard to get.
   a. deny b. demonstrate c. disguise

9. The tiger would make a good pet if we could only **domesticate** him.
   a. tame b. enslave c. dominate

10. If the Government cannot find a way to **stabilize** prices, it will be faced with runaway inflation.
    a. hold steady b. increase c. decrease

WORKING WITH WORDS:
Abjure and **adjure** share a root, which means "to swear." Their difference in meaning depends upon their respective prefixes. **Ab-** means "away from" or "off." Someone who **ab**jures something renounces it or "swears it off." **Ad-** means "to," and the original meaning of **adjure** was "to swear to" something. Today, if you adjure someone, you command him solemnly or entreat him earnestly to do something. Remember this sentence:

The judge **adjured** the criminal to **abjure** his vices.

Use the proper item of this confusing pair in the blanks below:

1. Cordelia ________________ all claim to her father's lands.

2. Before a boy can join our club, he has to ________________ allegiance to any other similar club.

3. Their Puritan father ________________ his sons never to touch alcohol.

4. The minister ________________ his congregration in the name of God to confess their sins.

B Write a form of one of the lesson words in Activity A in the blank space in each of the sentences below.

1. Lynne loved Nathan, and we didn't want to ________________ her, so we did not tell her that he was a rotten egg.

2. The UN mediator asked the nations to ________________ violence as a means of settling their differences.

3. It is possible to ________________ zebras and use them as workhorses.

4. Everyone ________________ with the parents of the boy who drowned at sea.

5. "You do not ________________ very well," she said. "I know you truly hate me."

6. We have successfully proved that cigarette smoking ________________ with lung cancer.

7. The doctors had to ________________ her blood pressure before they could operate.

8. We have ________________ our paper supply and will have to write on slate.

9. The mother ________________ her son to give himself up to the police.

10. He was unwise to ________________ a man of such high moral principles.

WORKING WITH WORDS:
It is often a good technique to try to determine the meaning of words by looking for words within unknown words. Consider the word **commiserate**. If you look at it closely, you will discover that it has within it a word very like **misery**. Knowing also that **com-** means "with," you could make an educated guess that the word means "to share misery with," "to sympathize with." List below other words from this lesson that are examples of words within words.

1. ________________

2. ________________

3. ________________

4. ________________

5. ________________

LESSON 11 misnomer nomenclature ascetic caption caucus harbinger palliative reprobate retrospect vertebrate

ver·te·brate

A Each of the following sentences contains a noun in **bold type**. Try to determine the meaning of the noun from the context; then write a possible meaning in the space provided. Check your answers in a dictionary.

1. "Skinny" is certainly a **misnomer** ________________ for Norma, who weighs 200 pounds.
2. Since there are names for every part of the body, it is not an easy task for a student of human anatomy to master the **nomenclature** ________________ of the field.
3. After he had seen much suffering, the wealthy man gave away his money, lost his desire for food and comfort, and became an **ascetic** ________________.
4. The photograph of the baseball team had a **caption** ________________ that listed the names of the players represented.
5. There was so much confusion among the delegates that the chairman called a **caucus** ________________ to discuss the issues calmly.
6. Throughout its range, the familiar red-breasted robin is considered a **harbinger** ________________ of spring.
7. As yet, nothing can cure a cold, but some cold remedies may act as a **palliative** ________________ on its symptoms, making one feel better.
8. That old **reprobate** ________________ has no respect at all for morality; he recently let his grandmother take the blame for a crime he committed.
9. In **retrospect** ________________, many wish the United States had not designed and used the atomic bomb; but at the time it was used, the act was praised as a way of shortening the war.
10. Many **vertebrates** ________________, including man, have a large supporting skeletal system in addition to the characteristic backbone.

WORKING WITH WORDS:
The key root of the first two words above is the Latin root **nomen**, which means "name." The root is also spelled "nym" in some words. Write the definitions of the following "name" words in the blanks.

1. nominee ________________________________
2. denominate ________________________________
3. patronymic ________________________________
4. pseudonym ________________________________

B Write a form of one of the lesson words in Activity A in the blank space in each of the sentences below.

1. All the nominees in the primary election attended the party ________________ to mingle with the various party members and officials.
2. The political cartoonist believed that the import of his caricature was obvious enough without a/an ________________.
3. The archaeological expedition discovered the bones belonging to an ancient ________________ and dated them at the time of the dinosaurs.
4. Although it seemed at first as if he had evolved a new theory, it turned out that he had merely devised a new ________________ for an old theory.
5. Many Christian monks are dedicated ________________, living lives of austerity and hardship.
6. "God will even allow a/an ________________ into His kingdom," the minister said, "if he will repent in time."
7. On her first trip to the zoo, my little sister committed a ________________ when she called a zebra a horse.
8. Looking back on his life in ________________, the old man regretted that he had invested his money unwisely.
9. The smell of the turkey from the kitchen was a/an ________________ of the delicious holiday feast to come.
10. Cold water is the best ________________ for burns.

WORKING WITH WORDS:
Most of the nouns in this lesson may be used either as verbs or as adjectives. Decide which word belongs in each of the blank spaces below. Write the word in the blank space, and after it write either "A" (for adjective) or "V" (for verb).

1. My cousin intends to study ________________ anatomy when he goes to college.
2. The Dada artist ________________ed his drawing of a spark plug "American Woman."
3. Our group will ________________ in room 211 as soon as everyone has finished eating lunch.
4. "The ________________ life is not the life for me," said the jolly, fat, fun-loving reprobate.
5. The minister ________________ed the evil act in the strongest terms.
6. What will ________________ the coming of the fall colors now that every tree on the farm has been cut down?

LESSON 12 choleric avid baleful brazen convivial fortuitous inordinate malleable palpable recalcitrant

malleable

A Each of the following sentences contains an adjective in **bold type**. Study each sentence carefully to determine the meaning of the word. Below the sentences are ten definitions. Choose the definition that goes with each **bold** word. In the space before each definition, write the number of the sentence in which the word it defines appears. Check your answers in a dictionary.

1. Ed is very **choleric** when he is playing cards; he throws his cards on the table whenever he gets a poor hand.
2. Nick is such an **avid** fan of the Phillies that he goes to every home game.
3. The monster gave us such a **baleful** stare that we shrank back in response.
4. The child was so **brazen** that even after his mother had just punished him he took still another cookie out of the jar right before her eyes.
5. Ted joined a fraternity because he enjoyed the **convivial** parties that they had.
6. His going to the party was quite **fortuitous**; he had planned to go skiing, but his friends swept him along with them.
7. The monkey in the zoo had such an **inordinate** love of peanuts that he ate himself sick every day.
8. The **malleable** mind of the child is relatively easy to influence.
9. The cause of her death was **palpable**—there was an empty bottle of sleeping pills next to her bed.
10. The **recalcitrant** protesters threatened to burn down the building if the president wouldn't come out and speak to them.

A. ______ menacing

B. ______ unplanned

C. ______ obvious

D. ______ bold

E. ______ excessive

F. ______ bad tempered

G. ______ capable of being altered

H. ______ rebellious against authority

I. ______ sociable, festive

J. ______ enthusiastic

WORKING WITH WORDS:

In medieval times, there were thought to be four fluids or "humors" in the body—choler, blood, phlegm, and black bile. The fluid which dominated was supposed to determine the character and general health of a person. From this theory, we have inherited the words for the four temperaments: choleric, sanguine, phlegmatic, and melancholic. Check your dictionary for the modern meaning of these words and use each one in a brief sentence.

1. ______________________________

2. ______________________________

3. ______________________________

____

4. ______________________________

____

B Write a form of one of the lesson words in Activity A in the blank space in each of the sentences below.

1. Though we may think medieval peasants were powerless, there is a case on record of a/an ________________ group hanging a king for refusing them the right to keep dogs as pets.

2. Martha wore a bathing suit to school, and the principal said she would be severely punished for such a/an ________________ act.

3. My ________________ old grandfather was constantly in a rage.

4. Every year at Christmas all my relatives get together for a/an ________________ feast at our house.

5. After being hit with a brick, he had a/an ________________ bump on his head.

6. Wilson is such a/an ________________ lover of tennis that he had a court built in his backyard.

7. Hal has a/an ________________ fondness for women and has married six of them.

8. We bought a police dog rather than a collie because the former looks more ________________ than the latter and thus makes a better watchdog.

9. The ________________ arrival of a policeman on the scene caused the boys to desist from their prank.

10. He wanted to marry a girl who was ________________ enough to be molded by him into a perfect housewife, but he couldn't find one.

WORKING WITH WORDS:
Below are six sets of words. In each set you will find a word from this lesson, followed by three synonyms and one antonym. Circle the antonym in each set, and be sure you know the meaning of each of the words. Check your answers in a dictionary.

1. **brazen:** impudent, diffident, shameless, brash
2. **convivial:** reserved, jovial, blithe, sociable
3. **inordinate:** exorbitant, immoderate, unreasonable, temperate
4. **malleable:** inflexible, pliable, ductile, tractable
5. **palpable:** perceptible, discernable, subtle, appreciable
6. **avid:** fervid, zealous, indifferent, keen

Review 4

Write one of the words listed above each set of paragraphs in the blank spaces below. You might have to alter the form of some of the nouns by making them plural or of some of the verbs by adding **-s** or **-ed**.

misnomer	**vertebrate**	**nomenclature**
convivial	**domesticate**	**defame**
malleable	**disillusion**	**palpable**
	commiserate	

I do not wish to (1)________________ science, but those who devised the (2) ________________ of the science of anatomy could not have seen our cats. If they had, they would have considered it something of a/an (3)________________ to call a cat a/an (4)________________. There is no (5)________________ sign of a back-bone in them. Cats are as (6)________________ as putty, and if you think there is a box of any size or shape into which a cat cannot fit, you will soon be (7) ________________ if you put it to a test.

It is also a mistake to call the cat a domestic animal. I (8)________________ with anyone who has ever tried to (9)________________ a cat. If you feed and water it well, it may be (10)________________ enough to stay in your house, but in a cat's imagination, a house is not a home but a jungle.

avid	**brazen**	**choleric**
ascetic	**dissemble**	**caucus**
baleful	**stabilize**	**adjure**
	reprobate	

A cat is no (11)________________; indeed so fond is he of good living that sometimes only the best food will satisfy him. He is also such a/an (12)________________ and so (13)________________ that he will come up on the dinner table and eat the food from your plate, even if you (14)________________ him not to. A cat also (15) ________________ well: if he wants to eat more than you have just fed him, he can act as if he hadn't had a meal in days.

Normally, cats are not (16)________________, but they can be upset, particularly by dogs with (17)________________ growls who think it is their business to (18) ________________ the household by keeping cats in their place. We have such a dog. At one point he became so obnoxious that the cats held a/an (19)________________ to determine how to deal with him. Recalling the dog's (20)________________ love of chasing mice, they bought him a mechanical mouse as a Christmas present and he has been chasing it ever since.

caption	**retrospect**	**fortuitous**
correlate	**recalcitrant**	**deplete**
harbinger	**palliative**	**abjure**
	inordinate	

The arrival of nearly all of our five cats was entirely (21)________________. We simply found them outside our door one day, meowing innocently, as if they were not the (22)________________ of chaos that they turned out to be. It was as if they were wearing a little (23)________________ reading, "Please feed me — I'm sad and hungry." After the fifth one arrived in this manner, I (24)________________ stray cats forever, lest they (25)________________ our financial resources entirely.

In (26)________________, however, I have to confess that we have gotten a/an (27)________________ amount of pleasure out of our cats. Even when they have been most (28)________________, they have been lovable and they have often served as (29)________________ in our more somber moods. We have come to believe that a love of cats (30)________________ with a love of independence.

LESSON 13 avow commute inaugurate align enfranchise enunciate whet ameliorate segregate transcend

**E•
NUN•
CI•ATE.**

A Each of the following sentences contains a verb in **bold type**. Try to determine the meaning of the verb from the context; then write a possible meaning in the space provided. Check your answers in a dictionary.

1. Gretchen **avowed** ________________ her dislike of her stepparents right to their faces.
2. He **commutes** ________________ to his job in the city every day by train.
3. We **inaugurate** ________________ a new President every four years, in January.
4. Although Smith was a Republican, he **aligned** ________________ himself with the Democrats on economic issues.
5. The National League decided to **enfranchise** ________________ a new baseball team in Toronto.
6. Coleridge and Wordsworth **enunciated** ________________ a new theory of poetry in their preface to "Lyrical Ballads."
7. Mr. Davis liked to have a cocktail before dinner to **whet** ________________ his appetite for food.
8. The parents were grief stricken by the death of their daughter, and nothing that anyone said or did could **ameliorate** ________________ their misery.
9. As long as we continue to **segregate** ________________ people, it is unrealistic to expect racial harmony.
10. Many great athletes have been handicapped in one way or another, but they have learned how to **transcend** ________________ their limitations.

WORKING WITH WORDS:
Among the many synonyms of **avow** are **acknowledge, allege, aver, concede,** and **confess**. Which of these words would you use in the blank spaces below? Check the accuracy of your answers in a good dictionary.

1. After the witness had been pressed by the lawyer for thirty minutes, he finally ________________ that he did know the defendant.
2. Sandy ________________ that her testimony was true.
3. He ________________ to the crime so that he would not have to stand trial.
4. Peter ________________ that he himself was the culprit and begged to be forgiven.
5. The police ________________ that the judge was in the pay of the gangsters, but they offered no proof.

B Write a form of one of the lesson words in Activity A in the blank space in each of the sentences below.

1. This year's school election is over, and the new student council officers will be ________________ tomorrow.

2. Because he liked to ________________ himself with winners, he always voted for the candidate who was ahead in the opinion polls.

3. My father disliked the train so much that he decided to ________________ by taxicab.

4. In his State of the Union message, the President ________________ a new foreign policy.

5. She is a great tennis player because every set she loses only ________________ her desire to win.

6. What can we do to ________________ the unhappiness of the poor?

7. Athletic teams are usually ________________ on the basis of sex.

8. Let's ________________ a new company to serve refreshments in the State Park; the prices of the old company are too high.

9. The priest ________________ that he believed in the concept of original sin.

10. In many ways, Lincoln ________________ not only himself but also his own culture.

WORKING WITH WORDS:
Several of the words in this lesson may be used in senses different from their uses in Activities A and B above. Determine which of the words from this lesson should be used in the blank spaces below and write the words in the spaces provided.

1. The Governor has the power to ________________ the sentence of a criminal.

2. You'll never carve that turkey unless you ________________ the knife first.

3. We are going to ________________ a new Asian policy as soon as we have conferred with our allies.

4. The Nineteenth Amendment to the Constitution ________________ women.

5. The students were ________________ alphabetically.

LESSON 14 colloquy aborigine accouterment amenity appurtenance exigency histrionics ramification retribution schism

SCHISM

A Each of the following sentences contains a noun in **bold type**. Study each sentence carefully to determine the meaning of the word. Below the sentences are ten definitions. Choose the definition that goes with each **bold** word. In the space before each definition, write the number of the sentence in which the word it defines appears. Check your answers in a dictionary.

1. At our school, we have instituted a bi-monthly **colloquy**, at which seniors and guidance counselors discuss careers.
2. The anthropologist wanted to talk to an **aborigine** of the region, not to someone from the tribe that had settled there recently.
3. Can one tell a duchess by her **accouterments**, such as jewels and dress?
4. The **amenities** of the club are what prompted me to join it; it is a comfortable and agreeable place to be.
5. The Commissioner was angry when the legislature voted to take away from him his chief **appurtenance**—a limousine.
6. The National Security Council was called into session to discuss the **exigency** presented by the firing of a missile on Florida.
7. His **histrionics** are merely a way of gaining attention; after he calms down, you'll be able to talk to him.
8. If he had foreseen that one **ramification** of the plan involved physical danger, he never would have acquiesced.
9. According to some Christian doctrines, **retribution** will come in the afterlife—heaven for those who have been good, hell for the others.
10. The minister said that all **schism** must end and the church must become united again.

A. ______ pleasantness

B. ______ trappings

C. ______ consequence

D. ______ native inhabitant

E. ______ formal conversation

F. ______ behavior exaggerated for effect

G. ______ a pressing situation

H. ______ punishment or reward

I. ______ separation or division

J. ______ a right or privilege

WORKING WITH WORDS:
Colloquy comes from a Latin root, **loqui**, which means "to speak," and a prefix, which means "together." A colloquy, then, is a conversation, though usually a more or less formal one. A related word, **colloquium** (plural, **colloquia**), refers to a more informal conversation or to an academic seminar on a broad field of study, typically led by a different person at each meeting. A **colloquialism** is an expression typical of informal or conversational speech. Write one of these related words in each of the blank spaces below.

1. In the fourth meeting of our ________________ last night, Dr. Peterson used the ________________, "bend his ear."

2. When the doctor called his colleagues together for a ________________, he sprinkled his speech with ________________s to show he was a "regular guy."

B Write a form of one of the lesson words in Activity A in the blank space in each of the sentences below.

1. Our penal system sometimes seems more interested in ________________ than in promoting criminal reform.
2. Among the ________________ of army generals are chest ribbons.
3. A/An ________________ of any modern President is his helicopter.
4. At a ________________ among the members of the political party it was decided to elect a new leader.
5. The ________________ split the Indian nation into two warring tribes.
6. The last ________________ of the primitive tribe died at the age of 120.
7. One ________________ of ending the military draft has been a great decrease in the number of college-trained men in the army.
8. One remembers Khrushchev's ________________, such as the time he took off his shoe and pounded it on a desk at a UN meeting.
9. We should have prepared for this ________________ by having an ambulance at the football field to take injured players to the hospital.
10. When I first moved to a rural area I missed the ________________ of city living, but now I prefer the country.

WORKING WITH WORDS:
Some of the words used in this lesson have special meanings in their plural form; others are more commonly found in the plural form than in the singular. Note the definitions below, and write the plural form of a word from this lesson beside its proper definition.

1. equipment used for a specific purpose or task ________________
2. social courtesies ________________
3. the original flora and fauna of a region ________________
4. urgent requirements ________________
5. equipment other than arms and dress issued to a soldier ________________

LESSON 15 ingenious ingenuous abstemious disaffected immutable ineffable inimical irrelevant unobtrusive unwitting

ineffable

A Each of the following sentences contains an adjective in **bold type** followed by three possible meanings. Circle the letter of the choice that comes closest to the meaning of the **bold** word. Check your answers in a dictionary.

1. The invention was so **ingenious** that the inventor was sure no one else had thought of it, and he rushed to patent the idea.
   a. clever b. excellent c. honest
2. Miranda is altogether innocent and honest; would the whole world were as **ingenuous** as she.
   a. beautiful b. insightful c. frank, naïve
3. It is difficult to be **abstemious** during a holiday season, when one is practically surrounded by so much good food and drink.
   a. hungry b. moderate c. uncheerful
4. There was so much false patriotism around him that honest Alceste became **disaffected** and went off to live on a deserted island.
   a. unfeeling b. alienated, unhappy c. forgetful
5. In time all things change, even the seemingly **immutable** hills.
   a. constant b. mighty c. coherent
6. She wanted to describe the emotions she had felt at the top of the mountain, but they were **ineffable**.
   a. too mysterious b. extraordinary c. beyond expression
7. Smoking cigarettes is **inimical** to good health.
   a. not effective b. harmful c. unjust
8. Many persons will vote against a candidate for a trivial reason in spite of the fact that such a thing is **irrelevant** to how good an elected official he may be.
   a. unimportant b. undesirable c. dishonest
9. Don't worry about the stain on the rug; it is so small that it will be **unobtrusive**.
   a. easy to repair b. acceptable c. unnoticeable
10. By opening a door for them, the guard became an **unwitting** accomplice to the crime.
    a. unintentional b. unlikely c. unwise

WORKING WITH WORDS:
Although there is only a vowel's difference between **ingenious** and **ingenuous**, there is a great deal of difference in their respective meanings. An ingenious person has an inventive and cunning mind; an ingenuous person is lacking in sophistication or is open, honest. Write the proper one of this confusing pair in the blank spaces below.

1. The boy from the country was so ________________ that city tradesmen were constantly taking advantage of him.
2. Da Vinci was among the most ________________ men who ever lived.
3. It would require an ________________ plot to steal the gold from Fort Knox.
4. At sixty-five, my grandmother was as ________________ as a three-year-old.

B Write a form of one of the lesson words in Activity A in the blank space in each of the sentences below.

1. Racial prejudice is ________________ to the wholesomeness of society.
2. Medieval monks tended to be ________________ in their habits.
3. In the face of the ________________ beauty of the landscape, we sat back in awe and wonder.
4. There is so much phoniness in the art world today that it is refreshing to find someone whose responses are truly ________________.
5. My uncle became the ________________ victim of the fraud.
6. At adult parties, children are supposed to be ________________, and if they are not, they may be put to bed.
7. The ________________ citizens organized their own republic.
8. I love detective stories with ________________ plots.
9. She said that all my reasons for wanting to marry her were ________________; the only thing that mattered was whether or not we were in love.
10. Her affection for him was as ________________ as the fact that day follows night.

WORKING WITH WORDS:
List in the columns below the prefixes from the words in this unit, the definitions of each, and a word not in this lesson that uses each prefix. Also be prepared to discuss what the prefixes have in common.

	PREFIX	MEANING	NEW WORD
1.	____________	____________	____________
2.	____________	____________	____________
3.	____________	____________	____________
4.	____________	____________	____________
5.	____________	____________	____________
6.	____________	____________	____________

Review 5

A In each group underline the word or expression which has a similar meaning to the first (**bold**) word.

transcend: cross, carry, pass beyond, overlook

amenity: pleasantness, desirability, amendment, awkwardness

ingenuous: obvious, candid, indirect, clever

schism: sarcasm, split, church doctrine, movement

enunciate: proclaim, deliberate, enable, endow

histrionics: study of history, nervousness, exaggerated behavior, unevenness

avow: discuss openly, denounce, avoid, confess

exigency: urgency, escape, exit, emergency

inimical: imitative, hostile, unusual, ill

segregate: separate, violate, victimize, destroy

commute: deliver, change, expect, explore

abstemious: absent, abnormal, alert, moderate

immutable: excellent, mute, hard, unchanging

irrelevant: isolated, unapplicable, silly, disagreeable

aborigine: abnormality, native, absolute, unfavorable

align: ally, alight, aid, assume

ineffable: lovely, inept, indescribable, inescapable

appurtenance: insult, excess, opportunity, accessory

whet: sharpen, whistle, watch, wrench

unwitting: dull, unable, unimaginative, unaware

B Choose suitable words from the list given below, and fill in the blanks.

The Governor ________________ed a/an ________________ policy intended to ________________ the miseries of ________________ minorities. He first called some leaders into a/an________________ in a hotel room, where he would not be surrounded by the ________________s of his office and where his power would be more ________________. He then told them that he would submit a bill to ________________ all the children of minority parents only, down to the age of twelve. An obvious ________________ of the bill, if passed, would be to increase the voting power of minorities. The Governor hoped that this would serve as ________________ for past wrongs.

unobtrusive	**enfranchise**	**retribution**	**disaffected**	**ingenious**
ramification	**ameliorate**	**inaugurate**	**accouterment**	**colloquy**

C Replace each word or expression in **bold type** by a word from Lesson 13, 14, or 15.

1. He was tired of his friend's **exaggerated emotional behavior**.
2. Let's set up a series of **formal discussions**.
3. The peasant was as **naïve and open** as we thought he would be.
4. His objections were **beside the point**.
5. She was well trained in the **social courtesies** of life.
6. One match only served to **stimulate** his desire for more tennis.
7. Excessive exercise is **not conducive** to good health.
8. The King's son is **no longer contented** with his father's authority.
9. He loved to surround himself with the **outward forms** of his position.
10. Who put you in charge of **rewards and punishments**?
11. It is time to **induct into office by a formal ceremony** the new officers.
12. The president of the league **granted privileges to** a new team.
13. The scene was **beyond expression**.
14. He **acknowledged openly** his guilt.
15. The upper classes were **separated** from the masses in their society.

D Match up each word in Column A with a suitable word or expression in Column B.

A		B
unwitting	______	of the office
abstemious	______	eating habits
align	______	victim
transcend	______	idea
ingenious	______	limitations
appurtenance	______	oneself with X

E Find in Lesson 13, 14, or 15 a word which is derived from each of the following roots. Write it in the space provided.

trudere (L) — thrust ______

mutare (L) — change ______

exigere (L) — demand ______

facere (L) — make ______

enuntiare (L) — declare ______

tribuere (L) — grant ______

melior (L) — better ______

franche (F) — free ______

schizein (Gk) — split ______

LESSON 16 undulate inundate boycott gambol harangue quibble stereotype inculcate intercede inveigle

boycott

A Each of the following sentences contains a verb in **bold type**. Study each sentence carefully to determine the meaning of the word. Below the sentences are ten definitions. Choose the definition that goes with each **bold** word. In the space before each definition, write the number of the sentence in which the word it defines appears. Check your answers in a dictionary.

1. We observed the ocean waves, which smoothly and peacefully **undulated** in a westward direction.
2. The tidal waves threatened to **inundate** every house along the shore.
3. Shoppers were urged to **boycott** the store because its manager refused to hire members of minority groups.
4. The children and their pets **gamboled** playfully in the park.
5. The sergeant **harangued** his men for fouling up the drill routine.
6. Whenever I asked Mr. Dithers for a raise, he would **quibble** rather than give me a direct yes or no answer.
7. If you **stereotype** members of a group, you will never appreciate the great diversity among the individuals of that group.
8. Dictatorial governments have commonly used the schools to **inculcate** officially approved propaganda in the youth.
9. The boys were about to have a fight when the vice-principal **interceded** and settled the quarrel peacefully.
10. By coaxing and flattering her father, Charlene finally **inveigled** him into letting her have the car.

A. ______ frolic

B. ______ flood, swamp

C. ______ win over

D. ______ be evasive

E. ______ surge

F. ______ refrain by concerted action from using

G. ______ develop a fixed idea of

H. ______ act as mediator

I. ______ instill, teach by forceful urging

J. ______ speak vehemently

WORKING WITH WORDS:
Both **undulate** and **inundate** come from a Latin word, **unda**, meaning "wave." **Undulate** means to move in a wavelike motion; while **inundate** means to rise in waves, to overflow or flood. Do not confuse these similar words. Write the correct item of the pair in the sentences below, and note the somewhat figurative uses of each.

1. Her long hair ________________ down her back.
2. The switchboard was ________________ with complaints from irate viewers of the television show.
3. I love the Midwest prairies where the grasses ________________ smoothly as far as the eye can see.
4. The disc jockey was ________________ with requests for the new record.

B Write a form of one of the lesson words in Activity A in the blank space in each of the sentences below.

1. The fact that the witness ________________ made the lawyer suspect that she had something to do with the crime herself.

2. It is possible that we could get the warring parties together if Canada would ________________ .

3. We hope that some sense of patriotism will be ________________ by the constant use of the pledge of allegiance.

4. It is possible for an author to ________________ his characters purposely; this might happen in a satire, for example.

5. Judging from the many pictures I have seen on nursery walls, lambs must love to ________________.

6. The waves ________________ the sand castle and made the child cry.

7. Mr. Chavez urged everyone to ________________ grapes, then lettuce, on behalf of farm workers.

8. The principal ________________ the whole student body for twenty minutes because they had not shown respect to the guest speaker.

9. The lawyer finally ________________ the witness into telling the truth.

10. The usually placid lake ________________ under the strong breezes.

WORKING WITH WORDS:
Five of the verbs used in this lesson are also nouns. Write a sentence for each one in the blank spaces below.

1. ____
2. ____
3. ____
____
4. ____
____
5. ____
____

The other verbs in this lesson may be changed into nouns by adding an ending to them. In some cases, in fact, you may make **two** nouns out of the same verb by using two different endings. List these nouns below.

________________ ________________

________________ ________________

________________ ________________

________________ ________________

LESSON 17

perspicacity perspicuity accomplice anachronism charlatan clemency idiosyncrasy infraction lassitude predilection

anachro·nism

A

Each of the following sentences contains a noun in **bold type** followed by three possible meanings. Circle the letter of the choice that comes closest to the meaning of the **bold** word. Check your answers in a dictionary.

1. A person has to have a great deal of **perspicacity** to understand the complex economic problems of modern society.
   a. perspective   b. mental acuteness   c. persistence

2. George Orwell has often been praised for the **perspicuity** of his writing style.
   a. lucidity   b. loveliness   c. perfection

3. The job of the third **accomplice** to the crime was to watch for police.
   a. gangster   b. partner   c. overseer

4. Many have claimed that women's colleges are an **anachronism**; they should have gone out with high-buttoned shoes.
   a. discrimination   b. waste of resources   c. something out of its time

5. The **charlatan** claimed to be a doctor, but in reality he knew no more about medicine than a fortune-teller.
   a. faker   b. professor   c. counselor

6. The judge decided to give **clemency** to the offender because he had never committed a crime before.
   a. a light sentence   b. freedom   c. mercy

7. Nero's wife indulged in an expensive **idiosyncrasy**; she always bathed in donkeys' milk.
   a. characteristic   b. strength   c. legend

8. In football, a team is penalized for every **infraction** of the rules.
   a. misunderstanding   b. violation   c. failure

9. After playing tennis all morning, Wally was overcome by **lassitude**, and he rested for the rest of the day.
   a. dreaminess   b. injuries   c. loss of energy

10. Dolly had such a strong **predilection** for vanilla that she never ate any other kind of ice cream.
    a. preference   b. yearning   c. sympathy

WORKING WITH WORDS:
Perspicacity and its related adjective, **perspicacious**, refer to acuteness of perception or understanding. **Perspicuity** and its related adjective, **perspicuous**, refer to something clearly expressed or presented, something easy to understand. Try to keep these closely related words straight. Write one of them in each of the blank spaces below.

1. A good synonym for ________________ is "shrewdness."

2. A good synonym for ________________ is "clarity."

3. There was no question what the message meant; its meaning was quite

_________________.

4. A good teacher must be _________________ enough to know when his students are not following him.

B Write a form of one of the lesson words in Activity A in the blank space in each of the sentences below.

1. No one expects to get _________________ from a hangman.
2. Although some ballplayers can bat both right- and left-handed, most have a/an

   _________________ for one or the other.
3. Although his employees never complained, the manager of the store had the

   _________________ to realize when they were dissatisfied.
4. Ben had not committed the robbery, but he freely admitted that he was a/an

   _________________.
5. Any serious _________________ of the honor code was punished by suspension.
6. Jane felt such _________________ that she didn't want to get out of bed.
7. The author is guilty of an _________________ in his latest book; his hero drives an automobile in the year 1850.
8. Great thinkers are perspicacious, but many of them are not known for the

   _________________ of their writing style.
9. Those who sell cure-all medicines are usually _________________.
10. Was it just a/an _______________ that drove Thoreau to the woods to live alone?

WORKING WITH WORDS:
In each of the sentences below, there is a word from this lesson along with two synonyms. Circle the word that fits best in each sentence and be prepared to defend your choices.

1. The man who pretended to be the King turned out to be a/an (charlatan, imposter, quack).
2. Her air of timidity was an (eccentricity, idiosyncrasy, affectation); she is usually quite self-confident.
3. His (lassitude, lethargy, stupor) was produced by too much alcohol.
4. The professor invited the (accomplice, colleague, partner) who shared his office to write a book with him.
5. He asked the priest to forgive his (encroachments, infractions, transgressions).

LESSON 18 covert overt ephemeral fatuous gauche sedulous specious virulent unctuous vicarious

A Each of the following sentences contains an adjective in **bold type**. Try to determine the meaning of the adjective from the context; then write a possible meaning in the space provided. Check your answers in a dictionary.

1. Drug pushing is usually a **covert** ________________ act, for if it were out in the open, it could be stopped more easily.
2. The intention of the writer was not **overt** ________________ because he did not wish the Government to know he was criticizing it.
3. The taste for black comedy in the theater that year turned out to be **ephemeral** ________________; not a single black comedy was produced the next season.
4. A **fatuous** ________________ person makes foolish remarks without realizing that they are stupid.
5. The peasant was straightforward but also **gauche** ________________; he ate with the wrong spoon and kept spilling things.
6. Many a **sedulous** ________________ secretary has never been properly rewarded for her earnest and painstaking care.
7. His argument seemed sound, but it was actually **specious** ________________; it was, in fact, altogether invalid.
8. The King should have known that the flattery of those around him was **unctuous** ________________, but he did not recognize insincerity in others.
9. I enjoy the **vicarious** ________________ thrills I get when watching a good adventure movie.
10. Rattlesnake venom is not always fatal, but it is a **virulent** ________________ poison, which quickly permeates the system of the victim.

WORKING WITH WORDS:
Covert and **overt** are opposites; to keep them straight, note the word **cover** in the former. Something that is covert is covered, concealed, hidden. **Overt**, in contrast, means open and observable, not concealed or hidden. Write the proper word of this pair in the blank spaces in the following sentences.

1. There is nothing ________________ in the behavior of an honest man.
2. The dictator said he had invaded the country to protect his own nation, but his true motives were ________________.
3. All our decisions are made in a/an ________________ manner, for we have nothing to hide.
4. A confidence man is not a/an ________________ person.

B Write a form of one of the lesson words in Activity A in the blank space in each of the sentences below.

1. He is so ________________ that I think I could use him to keep my hair in place.
2. His interest in reading detective stories was ________________, and he soon started reading much more serious fiction.
3. Her reaction to my proposal was unexpectedly ________________; she said she hated me and never wanted to see me again.
4. The scientist thanked his assistants for their long and ________________ work on the experiment.
5. Don't express your opinion in such ________________ terms; tell me plainly what you think.
6. The reflective look on his face bears a/an ________________ resemblance to deep thought; actually, he is in a stupor.
7. My grandmother enjoyed the ________________ experiences she got from watching soap operas on television.
8. John considers himself a philosopher, but I've never heard him make any remark that was not simply ________________.
9. Although he had read Emily Post, he had not digested her book and his behavior was extremely ________________.
10. One cannot always detect mental illness in a person from his ________________ behavior.

WORKING WITH WORDS:
Below is a group of eighteen words followed by six words from this lesson. Choose for each of the six words three synonyms from the group of eighteen. Write these words in the appropriate blanks below. Check your answers in a dictionary, and if your teacher asks, also check on the precise meaning of each of the synonyms.

assiduous	stealthy	artificial
synthetic	inept	ludicrous
evanescent	surreptitious	industrious
spurious	preposterous	clandestine
maladroit	fugitive	absurd
diligent	ungainly	transitory

1. covert ________________ ________________ ________________
2. ephemeral ________________ ________________ ________________
3. fatuous ________________ ________________ ________________
4. gauche ________________ ________________ ________________
5. sedulous ________________ ________________ ________________
6. specious ________________ ________________ ________________

Review 6

Write one of the words listed above each set of paragraphs in the blank spaces below. You might have to alter the form of some of the nouns by making them plural or of some of the verbs by adding **-s** or **-ed**.

inundate	**harangue**	**charlatan**
sedulous	**perspicacity**	**quibble**
specious	**perspicuity**	**ephemeral**
	predilection	

The (1)________________ of the thinking of the Greek philosopher, Plato, was matched by the (2)________________ of his writing style. Because of these qualities, his writings were not (3)________________ but have lasted to the present day. He was a/an (4)________________ worker, having produced over two dozen so-called dialogues that have come down to us.

The main speaker in most of the dialogues is Socrates. He sometimes (5) ________________ with his opponents in the argument to work them into his position, but he rarely (6)________________ them, preferring a calmer, more rational approach. Rarely, too, does he (7)________________ his listeners with a storm of words. His (8)________________ is for a series of questions, what has become known as the Socratic method. Though Plato's Socrates is not a/an (9) ________________, he sometimes uses (10)________________ arguments, which he then exposes as fallacious.

gambol	**inculcate**	**accomplice**
gauche	**stereotype**	**covert**
fatuous	**infraction**	**overt**
	lassitude	

Plato's theories of education are expressed in his dialogue, "The Republic." There was to be little time for children to (11)________________ about playfully. Although (12)________________ schooling was not to begin until a child was six, a kind of (13) ________________ education began much earlier. During this period, children were to be (14)________________ with accepted ideas of religion and patriotism. Formal schooling for many was to end at eighteen, when a series of examinations separated the workmen from the two upper classes. Plato tended to (15)________________ people fairly rigidly, but his schemes were by no means (16)________________, and he recognized that children born in one class might be promoted into another. And